BEING OUR OWN HEROES

BEING OUR OWN HEROES

Our Stories and Other Myths

THE TIMELESS AND TRANSCENDENTAL (TNT) BUNCH
Margaret Ashelman
Dorothy M. Beal
Fern Fairiebell Flesner
Harriet Glubka
Paul Godsman
Cielle Kollander
Hoshea Love
John Ong
Inez Valentine
Susan R. Wilk

∎

Edited by Linda Egenes

AUSTIN • FAIRFIELD • DELHI

BEING OUR OWN HEROES: OUR STORIES AND OTHER MYTHS. Copyright © April Fools Day, 2004, by the TNT Bunch (Margaret Ashelman, Dorothy M. Beal, Fern Fairiebell Flesner, Harriet Glubka, Paul Godsman, Cielle Kollander, Hoshea Love, John Ong, Inez Valentine, Susan R. Wilk and Linda Egenes). Printed in the United States of America. All rights reserved. No part of this book may be reproduced in any form or by any electronic or mechanical means including information storage and retrieval systems without permission in writing from the publisher, except by a reviewer, who may quote brief passages in a review.

LCCN: 2004110221
ISBN: 1-59540-985-8

Cover photograph © Lin Mullenneaux, 2003.
Book Cover and Design by Shepley Hansen.

WHO'S IN THE COVER PHOTO: Back row, left to right: John Ong, Ann Anderson, Paul Godsman, Inez Valentine, Linda Egenes, Cielle Kollander. In middle of picnic table: Susan R. Wilk. Front row, left to right: Fern Fairiebell Flesner, Margaret Ashelman, Harriet Glubka and Dorothy M. Beal. Missing from photo: Hoshea Love.

Published by 1st World Library—Literary Society, 1100 N. 4th St., Fairfield, IA 52556. First Edition.

Readers interested in supporting literacy through sponsorship, donations or membership please see our website at www.1stworldlibrary.org. or email us at literacy@1stworldlibrary.org.

*To our families and our peers
around the world*

Acknowledgments

We couldn't have done it without Linda Egenes. She was so much more than our teacher. She was a mentor and guide, expanding our abilities and horizons. We can't thank her enough, ever. Shepherd of her motley flock, she made suggestions or asked questions that encouraged us without shaking our sometimes wobbly self-confidence. Her delightful sense of humor and relaxed, loving style helped her doubting lambs frolic. The short pieces that follow are some of our gambols.

Thanks, also, to Lin Mulleneaux for the fun cover photo, Bill Beal for all-around support and taxi service, Keith Wegman for scanning the photos and lending technical support, Hap Mulleneaux for touching up the photos, Mary Zeilbeck for editing, Fran Clark for proofing and Shepley Hansen for creating our beautiful cover and book design. We are grateful to Rodney Charles and everyone at 1st World Library for believing in our book and making it happen.

Contents

Introduction 13

I. JUST KIDDING AROUND 17

The Dress-Up Trunk
Dorothy M. Beal 19

City Girl Discovers the Country
Dorothy M. Beal 21

My First Round-Up
Fern Fairiebell Flesner 23

Our Chickens
Fern Fairiebell Flesner 27

Growing Up on the Farm
Harriet Glubka 31

Teaching by Example
Harriet Glubka 35

SO BIG
Cielle Kollander 37

My Independence Day
Cielle Kollander 41

Scenes from When I Was Four Years Old and Older
Susan R. Wilk 45

Barefootedness
Susan R. Wilk 49

Uncle Willard Lyon
Margaret Ashelman 51

Hands Up
Margaret Ashelman 53

II. ALL IN THE FAMILY 55

My Mother
Fern Fairiebell Flesner 57

My Grandmother's Story
Inez Valentine 59

Reunion
John Ong 63

An Acquaintance with Books
Hoshea Love 67

III. GROAN-UPS 71

Cherchez la Femme at Eighty
Margaret Ashelman 73

Learning by Ordeal
Harriet Glubka 75

Acting Again
Dorothy M. Beal 77

Laughin' Man
Dorothy M. Beal 79

CONTENTS

PCS
Paul Godsman 81

Like the Power of Angels
Inez Valentine 85

Turning Point
John Ong 89

IV. RUN OVER BY KARMA 91

The Midnight Ride
Harriet Glubka....................................93

Model T Ford
Paul Godsman 95

The Ride
Hoshea Love 99

Silver Streaks and Fiery Dragons
Cielle Kollander 105

My Cancer
Fern Fairiebell Flesner..............................111

Recovering
John Ong 115

The Ultimate Adventure
Inez Valentine 119

V. MEET THE TNT BUNCH 121

Introduction

What started as a meeting of minds quickly became a melting of hearts. What did I expect at our first gathering, a continuing education class in memoir writing?

I knew, of course, that these students would be seekers, though not of my own 60s generation. These were people of my parents' age, who had families and careers and a whole lifetime of friends—and then somewhere in midlife started over in this community of meditators in Fairfield, Iowa, to help create world peace.

I didn't anticipate how deeply they would connect to writing. Each of their stories, so simple, so honest, revealed deep truths of life. I could never have predicted how stimulating, how rewarding and how fun it would be to teach them. These students' minds were settled and alert. Instructing them was like dropping a stone in a quiet pond—the ripples reached the far ends of the universe and bounced back with even greater power.

There was something magical about our meetings—a sharing of our true natures, both human and divine. As they wrote their life stories, they discovered a thread lightly stitching the past with today and tomorrow. They were able to see more clearly the higher purpose in all the events, people and places that were woven into the fabric of their lives. As they wrote their stories, they began to perceive their lives as more whole—and even heroic, as John pointed out.

Perhaps the nicest surprise was finding this group freer and less afraid to be themselves than other classes I've taught. After so many years of accommodating others on this planet, they were ready to stand up and be heard, to sing the song of their Self, no matter who was listening. Each wrote with personality, with an authentic voice—which is undoubtedly the most important and difficult writing skill to master.

Sometimes in class we'd get the giggles, like the time Margaret reported with a straight face that she wanted her stories to appear under the pen name of a man. She wouldn't listen to our objections, but while reading aloud her latest story, so obviously written by a woman, she'd stop every few sentences and say, "Mmmm. Peter Ashton couldn't have written that. I'll have to take that out." I never did figure out whether she was serious or just pulling our legs, one at a time.

We've had tears, too, like the time Dorothy read Fern's "My Cancer" story to the group. Paul wrote the only car story that ever made me cry—a coming-of-age vignette about the abrupt end of boyhood.

One person's story often evoked a flood of memories from the group, as when Harriet's "Teaching by Example" caused everyone to recall their own family meals. Other times painful memories were shared. But always there was a sense of growth, of evolution, of healing, of triumph of the spirit.

There was much common ground—the memories of the Great Depression and World War II. Yet much diversity. Susan's childhood in pre-war Germany and her escape to Sweden, Margaret's early life in Shanghai as the daughter of doctor-missionary parents, Fern's stories of homesteading on the South Dakota prairie. There were people who politely raised their hands before speaking, and there was Dorothy, tirelessly admonishing others to speak up and be heard, for Pete's sake!

Memory, memoir, remembering. In Sanskrit the word for

memory is *smriti,* which in its deepest sense means to remember who you really are. To remember fully, then, means to regain the memory of your infinite Self, to enjoy the fullness of life, to flood your mind with light eternal.

Scientists tell us that aging brings more connections between the neuronal pathways of the brain. This may explain why wisdom grows with age. It also explains why our class discussions were so rich—with cross-references to philosophers, expressions in other languages, and our own personal experiences.

These writers will send you back in time to touch the plush velvet of a special dress, smell the smoke pouring from a Model T engine, hear the winds of a prairie childhood. The sounds, tastes, textures and, most importantly, the uncensored feelings of childhood are all there intact, waiting to be shared.

Somehow aging puts people more in touch with these formative memories—and at the same time makes them less likely to edit them due to modesty or self-consciousness. It's as if the bedrock experiences that form our lives become covered by the gritty sands of everyday life over the years. But if enough time goes by, the dirt settles, and once again reveals the pure, white stones of the youthful mind, and with it wonder and openness to life's beauty. Perhaps that is why old age is sometimes called a "second childhood."

Let me make it clear that these people aren't sitting in their rocking chairs reminiscing about a life that's basically over. Hardly. Dorothy is not only a newlywed, but she is rediscovering her love of theater after a dormant sixty years. She recently staged a performance (with Margaret, Harriet, Fern, Inez and John cast in starring roles). Harriet continues her career as a counselor; Fern has worked the last fifteen years at a university. Inez, a lifelong artist, has switched from oil painting to watercolor, "since with watercolors, shaking just makes it better." Cielle, who at sixty-four is a junior member of the group, is still teaching voice internationally. Both Cielle and John, who recently retired from a lifetime of university teaching at age seventy-five, are developing new careers as writers. Hoshea is knee-deep in a full-time degree program in sustainable agriculture.

Through these remarkable writers, I have glimpsed the future, and it looks bright. I invite you to share in their vision and to enjoy the insights they offer to readers of all ages.

—*Linda Egenes*
Fairfield, Iowa

I

JUST KIDDING AROUND

The Cooley sisters in Albany, New York, 1931.
Left to right: Janet, Barbara, Dorothy and Robin.

The Dress-Up Trunk
DOROTHY M. BEAL

We raced up the stairs. Free! We were free. Six-year-old sister Barbara, cousin Marcia the same age, three-year-old cousin Lois and four-year-old me. The two sets of parents were downstairs in the living room doing their usual Sunday afternoon talk, and we kids were free to dig into the dress-up trunk in the attic.

What riches we had accumulated. Aunt Mimi, the flapper, had donated her old dresses and beads; Dad had added parts of his World War I uniform and a German helmet complete with a spike sticking from the top. There were gypsy skirts, a black silk belt and parts of Halloween costumes. I couldn't wait until I would be big enough to wear those. The belt alone weighed several pounds. Last to come out of the trunk were the lacy undergarments that had been shed in the present liberated twenties.

Lois and I, the youngest, were limited in our choices due to our small size. Lois donned Dad's puttees, and with her Sunday dress she was quite a picture. I chose the leather helmet, the kind that flyers of those open-cockpit days wore. I had begun my admiration of Amelia Earhart, the daring woman pilot, and wished I had a white silk scarf to complete the effect.

Barbara and Marcia argued over Mimi's orange chiffon dress with its long string of beads to match. Both girls looked silly in the dress, which trailed the floor when it was supposed to show a naughty view of legs. Another dress and more beads were found. We began planning the play.

Amelia Earhart falls in love. No, no, that wouldn't do. Although movies were forbidden to us we had heard the name "Clara Bow." We decided Clara would fall in love with a German soldier. Barbara was Clara the first go-round, Lois the reluctant lover. "I won't wear that helmet," she said, but was overruled by superior six-year-old forces. I clung to my Amelia Earhart image, so they wrote me in as the pilot who whisked them away. Marcia, Clara Bow's stand-in, allowed that the first Clara had to change roles after ten minutes.

We trooped down to the living room. The parents tried not to laugh. The play went on for about five minutes, until the stand-in said loudly, "It's my turn." Confusion ensued. The parents, hoping to shorten the proceedings, agreed with the stand-in, and clothing was switched. The imaginary plane was off again with the loving couple, and the performance concluded. The parents applauded cautiously, since they had learned from experience that too much enthusiasm produced another play the same afternoon.

Thus four-year old Amelia Earhart, also known as Dotty Cooley, began her lifelong love of acting.

■

City Girl Discovers the Country

DOROTHY M. BEAL

At first, we girls thought our parents crazy to buy that country place at the end of the road. The indoor plumbing was outdoors—an outhouse in back and a bathtub on the side-porch filled with newspapers. The electricity in the kitchen was a single bulb dangling from the ceiling. The living room floorboards were rotting through.

We were city folk—Mother, Dad and the four of us girls. Because Mother's health had broken down after baby number four, Dad always tried to lighten her load by sending Barbara and me to summer camp. One good thing about buying this old wreck for a summer place—I would never have to go to camp again.

The first time we visited, I walked a little way from the house into a large field. I lay down in the tall grasses. Those golden grasses met over my face with the sun coming through. I prayed, "May I never leave here."

I lay in the field and gave my heart over to happiness.

■

Fern and her sisters at their farm between Edgemont and Hot Springs, South Dakota, 1924. Left to right: Dottie (age four), Marian (age three) and Fern (age five).

My First Round-Up
FERN FAIRIEBELL FLESNER

My mother's dilemma was a serious one. My father had been called away soon after we moved to our new farm in the foothills of the Black Hills. She was left with three little girls: my sisters, three and four, and me, five years of age. It was up to her to take care of us children and the farm animals, including the cows. We had no barns or fences yet, so the cows had to be turned out on their own every morning. Some of them had to be milked, which meant someone had to round them up by horseback every night.

Before she left to round up the cows the first afternoon, my mother prepared us for her absence by showing us where to get food if something happened to delay her return. The next step was teaching us how to light a fire in the stove. I remember crumpling up paper and placing it in the stove, then covering the paper with wood chips. How my hand shook as I lit a big kitchen match for the first time and watched the flames flare up. It was what I considered my first grown-up accomplishment!

My mother was not a worrier, nor was she being unduly precautious. The horse could stumble or step in a hole—or a snake could frighten him, causing my mother to fall off. Although all these things were improbable, my mother knew that if something happened, the nearest neighbor was a mile away and my father would not be home for several days.

The first day went by with my mother returning on schedule to three anxious little girls.

The next day she decided that I should be the one to go after the cows. I was elated. I was to ride on my very own horse that had been a gift from my Uncle Ward. Born on the same day I was, the horse's name was Fox, and I had ridden Fox around the yard and up and down the road in front of our house. But now I was going to do a grown-up job.

As I watched my mother fasten the saddle, I began to have a few doubts. But the thrill of the adventure took over and I felt excited. My feet wouldn't reach the stirrups even on their highest buckle, but I still had the saddle horn to hang on to. This would keep me from sliding off as we went up and down the sides of the canyons. As I rode off, I looked back and waved before trees hid my mother and sisters from view.

Soon I came to the path in the canyon that my father had made by dynamiting the rocks. It was not a smooth path, but better than the other side of the canyon, which had a steep bank but no path at all. I had never been on the other side of the canyon until now, and as I stopped to listen for the cowbells, I glanced up into the tree ahead and looked into the large, round eyes of an owl. He stared straight back at me. I was surprised and a little startled, as I'd been told that owls slept in the daytime. Perhaps I had awakened him. We stared at each other and then I moved on, thrilled to have been so close to this beautiful bird.

As Fox picked his way amidst the cactus and sagebrush, I caught sight of a small dog-like animal loping along in the distance.

I knew this was a coyote, like the ones I had heard howling at night. Their cries were eerie and frightening, causing me to cuddle closer to my sister in bed and cover my head.

I stopped again to listen and again heard silence. In that silence I could hear the creaking noise of the saddle expanding and contracting as my horse breathed deeply. I felt truly alone, yet felt no fear. To me this was an adventure that I would cherish.

I soon found the cows and when they saw the horse and rider, they all started for home. My mother and sisters were waiting and it was a happy homecoming. I knew from the look on my mother's face that I had done a good job. It was good to be back home again.

This took place over seventy-five years ago. I have gone back to the old farm and found all the beautiful pine trees that shaded our house and barnyard cut down, and the logs of our house taken away. All that remains is the stone fireplace, a lonely sentinel standing watch over memories of long ago.

■

Our Chickens
FERN FAIRIEBELL FLESNER

Our family raised about twenty chickens on our farm in the foothills of the Black Hills in South Dakota. They never wandered far from their coop although they were free to wander over the whole 160 acres of our land. One of the reasons, I'm sure, was that they would miss one of the feeding times that occurred twice daily.

The other reason was instinct, which told them there was danger out there. This was wild country. There were rattlesnakes, bull snakes, coyotes, bobcats and skunks, as well as hawks that flew over every few days. These predators were big enough to swallow the baby chicks whole.

A special chicken door was cut into the big door of the coop. It was opened first thing in the morning and closed after they came home to their roosts in the evening. They went to bed early like the wild birds.

I spent a lot of time watching them, sitting on my favorite rock, which was under a pine tree at the edge of the canyon. The rock was enormous and provided a comfortable lookout. I loved watching the chickens because they were so happy.

The hens sang as they strolled around the yard, looking and

acting like life was a happy adventure.

The rooster was definitely the boss. He was a magnificent creature with shiny tail feathers and a personality to fit his looks. Sometimes when two hens would disagree and start an argument, the rooster would come running with great indignation written all over him. The hens always took off in different directions and I never did get to see what would have happened if the rooster had not separated them.

The rooster was also the one who watched for hawks. He would call a certain sound and all the chickens would run under the trees, squat down and wait quietly until he gave the "all clear" sound. When the hawk signal came, all activity stopped and the mother hen spread her wings for the baby chicks to take shelter in her soft, downy feathers. Up to fourteen chicks could disappear completely and without a sound. Sometimes a baby chick would stick his head out and look around as if to say, "What's going on out here?"

Each hen had her own idea of when she wanted to be a mother, but it was always in the spring or summer. She would climb into one of the laying nests that were lined up on the wall of the chicken coop or in the barns and she would not get out. She laid claim to all the eggs in that nest. When you reached in to get the eggs, she delivered sharp, hurtful pecks that said very plainly, "Keep out!" to anyone who tried to take her eggs.

At this time my mother would fix the hen a special place where she could be alone for two weeks until all the eggs hatched and she would come out to show us her family. The hen was so proud of her babies and they followed her everywhere.

She would scratch the ground with first one foot and then the other. Then she would wait and watch while her babies searched for the goodies she had dug up. They were never disappointed and peeped happily, acting like she had uncovered a feast. Even though I could never see anything in the dirt, the baby chicks got very excited.

I loved watching our chickens and I feel sad that so many farm chickens today are never allowed to wander freely or enjoy life as a member of happy family.

■

Harriet with three of her brothers and sisters enjoying the blossoms from the snowball bush in front of their farm near Altura, Minnesota, 1921. From left to right: Harold Speltz, Evelyn Speltz, Violet Speltz and Harriet Speltz.

Growing Up on the Farm
HARRIET GLUBKA

The air is full of fresh smells after a summer rain in Minnesota. My sister Violet and I are squishing and squashing through the puddles, giggling and having a jolly time watching the lovely mud wiggle its way up between our toes. The birds are adding their melody to the joyous atmosphere. Once in a while an angleworm sticks its head out to see what the party is all about.

When we tire of that game, Violet says, "Let's play house." We search for burdock bushes with little balls encased in prickly burrs. We don't mind the pricklies. We start shaping these balls into furniture. We don't need nails or glue. The pricklies will do. Soon we have a whole set of miniature furniture for playing house outdoors.

After a while Mom calls us. She has just taken a tour of the garden. She says, "The potato bugs are feasting on our plants. If we're going to have potatoes for next winter, we have to get busy." We each take a can and—ugh—start to work, coaxing bugs off potato plants and slipping them into our cans. We are paid well for our labor, though. We get a penny for each can full of bugs.

Now, what to do with the bugs?

Violet says, "Let's have the boys do it."

By now it's milking time, so we visit the barn. The aroma of fresh milk is so inviting. Dad treats us to a few squirts right from the cow's teats into our open mouths.

To finish off the day, we enjoy a delicious meal of chicken, mashed potatoes, gravy and vegetables.

I *still* wonder what the boys did with the bugs.

Harriet (center) and her cousins Alice Kalmes (left) and Phyllis Kalmes (right) in Minnesota, 1928.

Teaching by Example

HARRIET GLUBKA

It's time for spring, but the chill of winter is still in the air. It doesn't matter. It's cozy and warm in the farmhouse kitchen, with the smell of wood burning in the kitchen stove. Mom is cooking up yummy, aromatic foods. She's not making rice and dhal, more like roast chicken, mashed potatoes and gravy, with carrots.

The potatoes and carrots have come from our fruit cellar, where they were packed in sand to keep fresh during the long winter season. Did I say "fresh"? In fact they're so wrinkled it's quite a trick for my sister and me to peel them. In spite of their long winter nap in the sand, Mom manages to make them taste delicious.

I'm watching her make the gravy. She's not "teaching" me to cook. She's not talking. She's not saying, "Take a small jar with a tight lid, put water and flour in it, and keep shaking until the lumps are all smoothed out." She's not saying anything. She has a lot to do. The food needs to be on the table, set for ten, when the menfolk come in from working. They're hungry as bears.

We sit down to eat. It's scrumptious!

That's the story I tell my kids years later when they ask, "How did you learn to make such good gravy?"

∎

Cielle (second from left) and her mother, brother Stevie and sister Esther sample the snow outside her father's family home in Virginia around 1943.

SO BIG
CIELLE KOLLANDER

Way, way off an airplane is humming. Bright red or yellow? I wonder. One of those with double wings, I'll bet. Like a bumblebee, buzzing. Circling somewhere way out there in that great big empty space. That blue, far away, way-up-high place. Bigger than anything in the whole world. A place so empty, so big, you feel tinier than the tiniest thing that ever was.

It's strangely thrilling, but a little scary too, 'cause it makes you feel the war out there. You like it somehow anyway. It's telling a secret. Something quiet. Something deep. It's telling you that something in the world is that big, that open, that high, that blue. A sky that free. It's everywhere but you can't touch it. But it's touching you everywhere. Wow! Does it ever end, I wonder. And right there next to it, or under it, or inside it, there's a quiet, inside place too. You know that place. It's close. Deep. A way-inside kinda quiet. It's really big too. And they're the same somehow. This big blue outside place. And this inside secret place. They're both humming and close. If you need to go somewhere fast, somewhere safe, well, you don't have to go anywhere, it's just there. You can be there, safe and happy. It's a kind of Heaven, I think.

I had to go to that place a lot. Especially when sirens would come screaming in the night. Your body shaking all over—holding your ears and eyes shut real tight.

It's 1944. I am four years old in San Diego, a major Navy Port during World War II. Things are happening. Loud things. Scary, dark things, like air raids and blackouts. Demands from somewhere—from someone important.

All the shades have to come down all over the house, *fast!* All over town. Maybe all over the world. You must block out the light. It has to be dark. Totally. No light allowed anywhere. There is danger out there, and it will come in and get us, if any of the light seeps out.

Men come. Banging on the door—banging and shouting in the middle of the night. "Turn off that light!" Some of the light must have seeped out from the tiny lamp my father left on at his study desk. Sirens and blackouts and shouts. "Get under the bed, kids. Lie down. Put your hands over your heads." Mommy and Daddy are so serious.

Under there, shaking. All by yourself. A puddle of quiet tears on the floor. Time to find that quiet place, where nothing can get you. Nothing can harm you there. Nothing!

And there's the radio. You can always turn on the radio. It was *my* radio really, 'cause I loved it the most. So it was mine. It was. *Really.* It was over there in the corner on the little table with the velvety, smooth, pink cover. Sometimes the same voices came out of the radio. Big loud voices telling everyone about scary things happening. Bad things "THAT COULD HAPPEN. RIGHT HERE. RIGHT HERE AT HOME!"

But—there was other stuff on the radio too, fun stuff, really fun.

I loved my radio. It was my magic box. Full of dreams, music and stories. It was like taking long rides on a magic train. It would take you wherever you wanted to go. How I loved it. "Sky King" with Penny and Clipper, and "My Friend Irma," and "The Buster

Brown Show" with Midnight the Cat and Froggy the Gremlin. "That's my dog, Tide, he lives in a shoe, I'm Buster Brown, I live in there too." Wow, was I hooked. Hook-line-'n-sinker! My little ear glued to the dreaming box. Listening and watching my own inside picture show. My head stuck right up into that box of wonders. 'Cause this was one place you were allowed to go. Here you could be anybody. Go anywhere. Do anything. You really could. That was my favorite—my favorite thing in the world to do. Turn on my radio and go for a magic ride.

And the fun, dancy music of the big bands:

"Grab your coat . . . and get your hat . . .
leave your worries . . . on the door . . . step . . .
just . . . direct your feet . . .
to the sunny. . . side of the street . . . ."

How I loved it all. Those stories. That music. Weren't they just great. They made the whole world bright and sun-shiny. A place you really wanted to be. A happy place. A place where your heart could rest unafraid. Your mind could make wonderful pictures on its own little screen. Riding on your own train. Going on those dreamy, mysterious journeys. And they could come true right inside of you.

Oh, how I loved my radio. It meant so much to me. I just knew someday I would be on the radio too. I even kinda liked the scary stuff. The scary news and stories. It was *all* exciting, 'cause it was on the R A Y D E E O Y E A H !

■

My Independence Day
CIELLE KOLLANDER

"May I help you?" It was '46 or '47, I don't know exactly, but the terrible, dark war was over. There was happiness in the air, and people were smiling. Even my mommy was singing.

The big lady behind the counter was smiling down at me from way up high. First time out on my own. Like an airplane, I was buzzing high in a clear blue sky. Boy, was I! I had one whole hour on my own. That's a long, long time, ya know. I was six or seven by now. It felt so good to me, 'cause I felt like I had forever! I bet you know what I mean.

Our little neighborhood store had all kinds of stuff besides groceries. You could even get hot lunches there. This grown-up lady was asking *me* what I wanted, what I would like to have for *my* lunch. Wow! I was excited. Grown-up. No one telling me what to do or what to choose. I could have what I wanted. Wowee!!!

"May I have a hotdog please ma'am?" I asked, almost in disbelief at what was happening to me, at where I was. We always had to be polite and say "ma'am" and "sir" to grown-ups. I hoped she could hear me. She was so far away up there. Well, by-golly, I wanted a hotdog. They smelled so good. I wanted mustard and mayonnaise. They were hot hot hot—ooo—and the buns were steaming. The smell—oh god—I wanted pickle relish. I wanted everything!

Choosing, buzzing, eating, listening to the sky, feeling it all around me and inside. Oh boy, *this* is Heaven for sure.

I had my own lunch money. Twenty whole cents. It was enough for everything. And I wanted a soda pop. I loved Grapette in those littler bottles, and Biyearlies Orange Drink. My sister and I and our friend Peggy—we sang commercials for them. We were on the radio. A singing trio. Yeah, it's true, we sang for Biyearlies and 7-Up too. So it felt like they were mine—my very own soda pops. And I wanted one, now.

So I walked over to the great big icebox in the corner, holding my hot dog carefully. Mustard was already dripping down my hand. I was trying to hold it just right. I didn't want to squeeze it too tight, or drop it. All that stuff on it made it big and fat. It was getting really heavy.

A boy had come in and opened that huge icebox door to get something for himself. It was so cold, fog was rolling out onto the floor like a cloud. "Can I have an orange drink?" I kinda whispered it, feeling a little shy 'cause he was a boy, and I didn't know him. Besides, boys were kinda scary—at least my big brother was sometimes. But he smiled and handed me a tall, cold bottle. It made my other hand freeze, but I didn't care. He smiled at me again and closed the cold, foggy door. "Thank you," I said quietly, nearly beside myself with his friendliness and my freedom. The saliva was filling up in my mouth. Was I hungry.

My last penny. Standing there looking through the glass at all that candy. Boy. I had a big choice to make. Abazabba, Bit-O-Honey, Black Jack, Beaman's, Bazooka, Double Bubble, Jaw Breakers IN SIX COLORS!, Sugar Daddies, Sugar Babies . . . Uhhh . . . I wanted them all. OK . . . let's . . . see . . . what's it gonna be? Mmm . . . ABAZABBA IT IS, YES! I loved the taffy of it. White taffy with that soft, gritty peanut butter melting down the middle thing . . . mmm . . . perfect perfect perfect. The perfect dessert to top off a perfect lunch on a perfect day.

I felt what a drunken bumblebee must feel. I was red and yellow. I must be. With at least two sets of wings. An airplane buzzing 'round those puffy little clouds in a sun-shiny sky. Just like in my color book. Nothing to do but just be sunny, happy and free as can be. I had tasted it, and it was dee-licious. My own bright, shiny freedom.

So I hummed and sang and buzzed my way, hop-scotching back to school. I was filled to the brim, with my first real taste of paradise fresh on my lips, and a song in my heart. I knew without a doubt that

"Life . . .
could be so . . sweet
on the sunny . . .
side of the street."

■

Scenes from When I Was Four Years Old and Older

SUSAN R. WILK

ONE

During my first six years in Gauting, near Munich, opposite our property there was a field, and behind that field lay a beech grove. When the beechnuts were falling from the trees, we would go there and indulge in eating those triangular nuts. Their shells were similar to hickory nuts. When you broke them open, you would find three or more tiny nuts with smooth, brown coverings that you needed to peel off. And then you had the little white nuts we treasured.

One time my brothers and my sister wanted to go there in autumn without me. But I was disconsolate, so they finally decided to let me come along.

What they had planned to do was to roll up some dry beech leaves like cigarettes and smoke them. I tried one, but I did not like the scratchy taste in my throat.

TWO

In our nursery we had a little table with chairs and a bench. One time before Christmas, my sister, who was three years older than me, was standing on top of the bench back, looking out the window. She said, "There goes the Christ child!" Our window was facing in the direction of the field, and at the right end of it was a large fir wood. It took quite some time for me to climb up the back of the bench to look out of the window. Then she said, "The Christ child just disappeared behind the corner. Only the train is still showing." Of course, I saw nothing!

THREE

One morning during the same year, I was standing on our terrace in front of a stone wall. Having watched my artist mother make paintings, sculptures, drawings and other works of art, I was inspired to do similar things. With a little piece of wood and my brother's pocketknife, I intended to make a woodcarving, when all of a sudden the knife slid down the wood onto my left-hand thumb. My sister said, "There grows wild meat!"

The village doctor was called. He arrived many hours later and sewed it up very badly. The scar is still to be seen.

FOUR

I always had confidence that I could do anything I wanted to do. When I was seven years old, as a Christmas gift for my father I made a little book with a poem for each season, except for the winter season, for which I had no inspiration. My father, being a scholar in art history, did not appreciate my early attempts. So in spite of earning good grades in school for my stories, I decided that my talents did not lie in writing!

Maybe my father should have encouraged me rather than

holding me back. I could have started writing many years ago—but at least here I am now!

∎

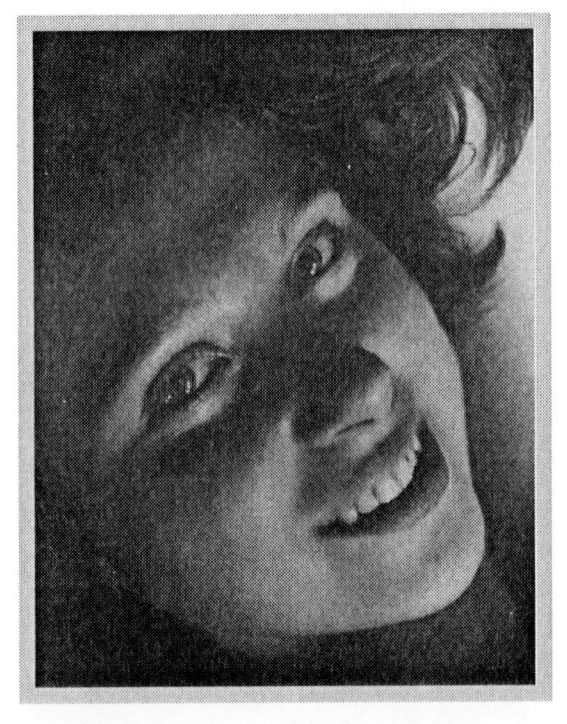

Susan at age twenty-four, Denmark, 1939.

Barefootedness
SUSAN R. WILK

Our house was on the high road, Amerseestrasse Three in Gauting, near Munich. The beautiful Amersee is a lake about twenty miles southwest of Gauting in south Germany. Its water is light green with the Alps as a backdrop.

Street cleaning did not happen frequently in Gauting. So when in the fall the leaves dropped from the trees that lined our street, clusters of dry, rustling leaves were fun to stir with my bare feet. But what I treasured most was walking through the puddles of water after the rain, and after most of the water had evaporated, walking through the mud that remained. It felt like walking on silk.

When I was four years old, my mother said, "Let's go on a walking tour to Unterbrunn. Susi, put on your boots!"

"Why boots?" I was thinking. I always walked with my bare feet. Besides, boots on my naked feet? I did not like that feeling. And besides, maybe I did not have socks or stockings after the war in the year of 1919. I decided to go as I was used to, with my bare feet.

It was autumn time and the grain had recently been harvested. What I did not know was that our walking tour meant crossing over a large stubble field. Every step I took hurt my feet.

Even after we had crossed the field, walking on the road still hurt. My feet were so sore. Tears were running down my cheeks all the way. About that outing I remember nothing, only my hurting feet. With tears in my eyes, I saw nothing.

Nowadays, during the very hot summer season, when indoors I enjoy walking barefoot, especially on my extremely soft and colorful rug. But outdoors, preferably, I wear sandals.

■

Uncle Willard Lyon

MARGARET ASHELMAN

Growing up in Shanghai, we children didn't see most of our real relatives, but adults we were fond of we called "Uncle" and "Aunt."

Uncle Willard Lyon wasn't my real uncle, but I did enjoy sitting on his lap when he told us stories. Only when I was much older did I realize that he liked doting on me, as his wife had to take their own young daughter to the United States for medical treatment. I don't remember any of the stories he told, but I enjoyed the sense of security and affection that accompanied his visits.

Much later I realized that my father was also very fond of me, but I don't ever remember sitting on his lap. My father was actually a better storyteller than Uncle Willard, and told us of his many adventures. As a public health educator, he spoke in Chinese to audiences all over the country, using small models of people and houses on moving belts to illustrate the benefits of covering food so flies couldn't land on it. I was impressed by his achievements, but I was afraid of my father, whose violent temper could erupt without warning.

Uncle Willard was gentle and safe. When we arrived in New York, he met us at the boat and took us to my first cafeteria. I did everything he did, even taking a small loaf of bread which I never would have had room to eat. He was a six-foot-three man with an appetite to match. Seeing how full I was just eating what was on my plate, he suggested we take the bread I had bought outside and give crumbs to the pigeons. No scolding for taking more than I could eat—only a chance to share our largesse with the birds!

Hands Up

MARGARET ASHELMAN

I was too young to talk much with anyone, even my own family, but I was born with exploring hands. While my mother and older siblings were eagerly talking with friends in the vestibule after church, I was quietly surveying the varieties of coats at eye level—from an adult's waist down. Such a variety of fabrics! And what was that near me? All black, but when I tentatively touched it, so soft. I didn't know that its name was velvet, but I found it so silky—alluring, in fact. One touch called for another, and soon my small hand began stroking it, oh, so quietly!

But not quietly enough. The wearer of the velvet coat looked down and recognized the small girl gently touching her coat. She was a wealthy donor to a Shanghai hospital, and my doctor mother was on the hospital board. I don't know whether my mother found me still feeling the coat, or the friend hailed my mother nearby, but the friend declared that a little girl who loved velvet so much should have an outfit made of velvet. She claimed it was an old coat anyway, and arranged to have her own French dressmaker make me a velvet dress with a hat and muff to match—all with pink silk lining and piping. Now I had a Sunday dress—so unusual for a daughter of a missionary—with such elegance and beauty that I remember it to this day.

■

II

ALL IN THE FAMILY

Fern's mother, Daisy Wrightson, in 1918, before marriage.

My Mother
FERN FAIRIEBELL FLESNER

In 1902 at age eighteen, my mother, Daisy Wrightson, traveled with her family in a covered wagon to Mead County, South Dakota. She continued by stagecoach to the town of Spearfish in the Black Hills to attend the teachers college in that community.

Her family in the meantime had founded a small community on the prairie. It consisted of a livery stable and blacksmith shop established by her older brothers, Harold and Ralph. Her older sister, Nellie, ran the post office while her parents served the customers at their country store, which sold just about anything that a settler's family might need.

This town, named Wrightsonville, remained on the map of South Dakota for many years, until a stroke of lightning set off a conflagration that burned it to the ground. The family members then abandoned the venture.

My mother taught primary school in available shelters that served as schoolhouses. At times claim shacks or sod houses served the need for a schoolhouse. Her life at that time was filled with challenges and related rewards for meeting those challenges. She boarded with some of her pupils and became part of their families.

She told me of one occasion when she was teaching in a claim shack and a rattlesnake decided to occupy it. Her efforts to deal with the snake were somewhat complicated by a student on the verge of fainting.

There were few fences or bridges in that area then and the roads consisted of well-worn buggy and wagon trails. My mother's pony, Rudolph, was her means of transportation and a trusty companion as well. He always knew the way home from wherever he found himself, even on the darkest of nights.

Mother married in 1918 and stopped teaching in 1919, when I was born. When my two sisters and I had grown a bit, she returned to the teachers college and later resumed her teaching career. She was very much in demand and taught in primary schools for twenty-six years on her beloved prairie.

She loved every season, especially the springtime with the song of the meadowlark, and even loved the winter with its blizzards, which she considered to be a challenge. On one occasion she spent two days isolated in a schoolhouse by such a blizzard.

She was truly a pioneer lady of the western prairie.

■

My Grandmother's Story
INEZ VALENTINE

Her name was Rebecca Jane Brinkley, and she was born into a family of five boys in North Carolina. Her mother was Cherokee and her father came straight from Ireland. During the Civil War, her five brothers hid in the mountains so they could avoid fighting. The black people of their town secretly brought them food in the middle of the night. As a result of this kindness, the family was deeply grateful to the black community, and thus sympathized with the North.

My grandmother's young husband was killed in the war, leaving her widowed with a two-year-old son at the age of eighteen. She was a convert to the Mormon Church, which her Southern Baptist family strongly opposed. To keep her from joining the Mormon pioneers, her brothers kidnapped her son and hid him. I imagine that she was frantic and didn't rest until she had found him. Her family couldn't stop her, though, and she soon joined the pioneers and crossed the plains to Salt Lake where she settled with her son. She married a polygamist, but after discovering this meant becoming a scrubwoman, she appealed to the leaders of the church and they granted her a divorce.

I didn't know her because she died about six years before I was born, but my mother told me many stories of her life. My grandmother later met and married my grandfather, who had emigrated from Norway. I didn't know him, either. But I did know Uncle Jess Barker, the two-year-old who crossed the plains with his mother.

If you are doing the arithmetic and have decided that there should be three generations between now and the end of the Civil War, it is easily explained. My mother was born when my grandmother was fifty.

■

*John Ong, Jr., at the reunion of the Bristol family, Tucson, Arizona, 1932.
Left to right: Orlando James (O.J.) Bristol, Amelia Fuhrman Bristol,
Lucille Bristol Ong, John Nathan Ong, Jr., John Nathan Ong, Sr.,
Polly Bristol, Polly Elizabeth Ong, Florence Bristol.
Photographer: Charles Moyer.*

Reunion

JOHN ONG

A rare photograph of my mother's family starts the flood of memories.

For my grandfather, O. J. Bristol, all his family was there—daughters, son-in-law and grandchildren (that's me in the center of things!).

I wonder why the picture was taken, I just wonder . . .

"It's just wonderful that we can all be here together in Tucson," says Florence.

"Especially since we haven't seen our sister Lucille for five years while she has been living the romantic wanderer's life in Spain," says Polly.

"Not only that," says their mother, Amelia, "but she's brought back two beautiful new ones—our first grandchildren!"

"I'm proud of your achievements," says O.J., the father of the three, to Lucille. "I admit that we were apprehensive when you made that long trip from Montana by train, boat and automobile to marry your husband in Morocco. We're overjoyed that all has worked so well with you and your husband, Jack."

"Why don't you and Charlie tie the knot?" Lucille asks Polly.

"We'd love to, but times being what they are in the United States in 1931, we just can't afford to right now," says Polly.

"Let's immortalize this occasion," says Jack.

"You're right," says Charlie. "I'll take the picture. Let's go outside. Let's see—Grandpa and Grandma on the left, Lucille next, John junior next to his Dad, then Polly holding her namesake, Polly, and Florence on the right. Hold still and smile, everybody!

CLICK!

What did these people come to mean to me?

My father, John (known as Jack by his contemporaries)—taciturn, with a subtle sense of humor, honorable and esteemed by his peers—a good role model.

My mother, Lucille—progressive, adventuresome, a gracious hostess, devoted to her family and friends. She would start her Christmas letters in October and write over one hundred of them! She had a strong sense of justice and was able to convince my father that their two daughters needed higher education, too.

My parents—I give them nine out of ten for parenting. We lacked for nothing, were not abused or terrorized and were given good educations.

My sister, Polly—a unique childhood shared, a lifelong friendship.

Each of them contributed to what has been, for me, a happy and fulfilled life.

■

Hoshea Love at age twelve, Lake Elsinore, California, 1951.

An Acquaintance with Books
HOSHEA LOVE

Life and living is wonderful to me, especially now that I know more about who, what, how and why I am. Like you, I am many persons or expressions, and I have many images. A simple way of seeing this is to note that a person is an individual—a male or female, an adult or child, a member of a family, an employee or student, a dad or mom, sister or brother—all at the same time.

And because we are so multidimensional, we experience all manner of feelings and exhibit a variety of behaviors. I feel each of us is a universe—a grand community. We're also an encyclopedia, a reservoir of knowledge, thoughts and experiences. That's why it's good to share our thoughts and stories, because in that way our identity and definition is maintained in balance, and our evolutionary progress is nourished.

Today I realized that I am a book person. On this day I have seen my reflection in the words written by Leslie Silko, a Pueblo author. The descriptions in several of her memoirs image me in detail: many things I wondered about, because in my past I had found no direct connection with human culture around me. Things like, Why do I have knowledge before I have learned? Why am I drawn more to nature and the universe as home, instead of my physical family? Why are my thoughts and feelings so different from others around me? I'm human like they are, but they speak and do things that seem strange to me. I can adapt, but I don't fit in. Somehow the world inside me is different, but I don't know why. The Spirit of Heaven and Intelligence of Nature are my parents, the universe my home and community. This is the knowledge that sits comfortably with me. All of nature is my family.

Elements of other written works also resonate with me, but I single out Silko's works because in them the connection is so strong. In them I see a clear reflection of how I have known myself to be. According to my family's oral tradition, I'm a composite: Cherokee and Irish from my mother, Blackfoot and African from my dad. My mother from British Columbia, Canada, my dad from Mississippi, USA.

As I reminisce I realize that I've always had an acquaintance with books from childhood on up. I remember *Dick and Jane* in elementary school and reading the *Beowulf* epic and the *Canterbury Tales*. And the Pop-eye and Olive Oyle books that circulated among the boys in my school. Oh, yes, and comic books. A Looney Toons addict, I was: Donald Duck, Bugs Bunny, Elmer Fudd, Daffy Duck. Oh, yes! Red Rider and the Lone Ranger, *Boy's Life* as a boy scout, hunting and outdoors magazines, and novels in the summertime. Sometimes for days I would do nothing else but read. I'm remembering now.

Yes, I recollect the time when the word "physician" got me a backhand from my mom. She became exasperated when I continued to mispronounce the word "physician," because she dearly wanted me to be able to read the Bible. She said all learned men knew what was written in the Bible. But that pesky word "physician" got my tongue tangled up every time.

For me it's a memory that vividly punctuates the importance of words. Ten years later, I finally got back to that book and read the whole of it. In later years, when my interest in family began to stir, I learned something my mother had kept secret. Mom told me she had always read the newspapers thoroughly and that's why she was able to get my older bothers and sisters to go to college. Because she was so well read, she gave them the impression that she had gone through college herself. But they found out later that she had only taken a few classes and never did complete college. She was a reader, especially the Bible. I think that gave her comfort.

∎

III

GROAN-UPS

Margaret Ashelman in 1972.

Cherchez la Femme at Eighty
MARGARET ASHELMAN

At this late date, several parts of me have decided they will no longer stay with the gang and want to set out on their own. Some of this mutiny is new, but the tendency has been either latent or bold for decades.

My skin has spots not arranged with charming design but quite unexpectedly on arms, legs and tummy.

My knuckles decide they are grown up now and keep swelling, trying to nudge out their neighbors as if they weren't on the same hands. How can the hands look as if they'd be delicious being held by an attractive man if these knuckles keep nudging each other just for attention?

My hips: I haven't been exercising them especially, but how come last season's slacks fit everywhere except around the middle? I can't even zip up the near-the-belly-button closures and have to wear blouses out so the uncompleted and discouraged front zipper doesn't show.[1]

Fortunately, I still wear the same shoe size and haven't worn heels since they went out of fashion for most people. The styles of my other clothes have come and gone—perhaps several times—but fortunately the clothes don't know it. I keep wearing them (I don't want them to feel like orphans). Even if all my friends recognize them, at least strangers don't!

Who cares if my hair grows more silvery year by year—at least I can go to plays from time to time rather than spending the money on hair dyes!

What about wrinkles? I've always called these on the outer edges of my eyes "smile lines." If there weren't a few wrinkles, strangers would guess the great-grandmother had indulged in a face-lift.

And I can rejoice that I am a woman. Most older men I know carry extra pounds like a sack worn in front. Women can buy muu-muus in Hawaii and wear those extra pounds anywhere—and we often do!

∎

---

[1] I'll tell you a secret. If you thread a rubber band through your buttonhole and latch the other end over the button, this gives you a certain amount of leeway. But of course, at some point it's hopeless.

Learning by Ordeal

HARRIET GLUBKA

I'm in the kitchen washing dishes, sort of listening to the radio at the same time. The announcer gets my attention when he says, "Learn to speak with ease before a group of people. Come to a meeting at the Winona Hotel at six this evening."

I hear the word "learn." Of course, that means I have to attend. I'm remembering back about thirty years, hearing my mother say in a moment of anger at her in-laws, "They think they're better than we are because they're better educated." My child mind interprets that to mean, "They ARE better—because they have a college education." Maybe that's when my psyche began to be infused with the idea that more education means "a better person." That belief influenced my life into my older years, long after I knew better.

Now the radio announcer is telling me the many ways in which my life will be more successful and happy if I go to the meeting and learn to speak with ease before a group of people.

WOW.

Promptly at 6:00 p.m. I'm at the hotel sitting at a large table with about thirty other women. We enjoy a delicious meal as I happily anticipate the next part of the program—a lecture on how to get over my stage fright about speaking before a group.

I soon learn, to my horror, that this is not to be a passive experience on my part, but "hands-on." (My friend Margaret, upon hearing me read this, interjects, "tongues-on.")

The emcee passes a basket containing little folded slips of paper, a possible topic for an impromptu speech written on each one. I want my chair to fall through the floor, or better, that I become invisible. But, alas, no such thing happens. Now I face a dilemma. Shall I refuse to take a topic and embarrass myself immediately, or shall I postpone the embarrassment until later by declining to speak when my turn comes? Maybe someone will yell, "FIRE!" and we will all run out of the building.

None of the above occurs. Suddenly I realize that the person next to me is sitting down after her little speech and, obviously, it is my turn. There seems to be no honorable escape, so I slowly rise to my feet with my knees shaking. I look at the sea of faces looking at ME.

The little folded paper I have drawn out of the basket is a cartoon. It shows a dejected-looking man in raggedy clothes sitting on a curb watching a limousine drive past with a uniformed chauffeur and a nattily dressed man sitting in the back seat. The raggedy man on the curb is saying, "There, but for me, go I."

With the little paper in my hand, I take another look at the audience. These women are smiling. They don't seem too scary now, so I speak.

I go home to the safe place in my husband's arms. He assures me that I am indeed good enough to join the group. I do join the newly formed Toastmistress Club and am eventually elected president. I stand on my feet, conducting meetings.

Never again will I be glued to my seat, thinking, "There, but for me, go I."

∎

Acting Again

DOROTHY M. BEAL

What is in my heart this morning is the possibility of acting again. What fun it was for me then. The question is not can I still do it in my eightieth year, but will it mean as much to me now? I started writing a lot this spring as a continuation of journals I had been keeping. The poetry that poured out this year was a flood that came from time to time. "Carefree Painting," as I call it, was and is a lark. Picking out chords on my new piano is a joy, but acting?

So I signed up for Rodney's one-week acting class. Whew! What an experience! Ten souls appeared, three fourteen-year-olds, three sixteen-year-olds—you know, kids. There were three middle-aged types and I, and we were off to the races. Stretch, stimulate and integrate. These exercises were repeated every day to make our voices come out better, and it worked. I felt tingling in every part of my body. Shakespeare's twenty-ninth sonnet had been our homework. Every day we did it singly, in the group, or we just recited our favorite lines. As we learned about the importance of vowels, we improved.

Rodney is an actor. His face is expressive. We watched him do what he called "kissy lips for ooo" and strained to do it. Our lips hardly moved. We tried to drop our chins for "ooo" and they wouldn't budge. We smiled big for the "eee" sound and grimaced.

I began to apply what I was learning to the second sonnet I had chosen. I remembered the reputation Shakespearean actors had for declaiming and tried it. It felt great. At home, husband Bill heard me declaiming and cheered. "You're getting out of your box," he said. I watched the other students. They began to climb out of their boxes, too.

One forty-five-year-old singer who was afraid to sing in public enthusiastically leaped to her feet to recite. The young math whiz who was locked up in his head began to stand squarely on two feet and speak it out. The faded lady, pale in face, voice and clothes, had color in her cheeks. She still whispered but looked happier. Even the high-school teacher, so organized in his notebook and so stiff in his body, began to relax and let it flow.

After the first day's session I was so exhausted I came home, ate, and slept for two hours. The second day I slept for just one hour and the third day I didn't need to sleep at all. By the fourth and last days I realized that my whole physiology was stronger and more enlivened.

There was a casual mention of auditions to be held the day after this course. "Auditions for what?" I asked.

"We will decide when we see who shows up," was the answer. Later I told Bill that I couldn't do it. The course had been a big thing for me and I needed to digest all I had learned. The expression on his face told me that quitting now was not a possibility.

So, where will I be this afternoon at one o'clock? You guessed it. The Spayde Theater again, ready for stretch, stimulate, integrate—and whatever else follows.

■

Laughin' Man

DOROTHY M. BEAL

I'm gonna get me a laughin' man
Soon as I can, my laughin' man
A laughin' and a huggin' and a sweet old man
Soon as I can, my laughin' man.

[This poem was written before Dorothy found her laughin' man and married him in 2002.]

∎

PCS

PAUL GODSMAN

In the military, the acronym PCS stands for Permanent Change of Station. For the military family this is a term freighted with implications of severed friendships, uncertainty, changes, and not the least—the stress of moving. This effect is multiplied many times over when it happens to an entire unit.

As I entered our quarters one noontime in mid-summer of 1955, I greeted my wife, Eloise, with the news, "Well, Gyroscope is on for Germany in January, but we will be going on the advance party in October."

"Tell me something new," she replied. "I heard that two days ago."

This took the wind out of my sails for a few moments, until she relented and explained, "Barbara Fuesel told me about it at the wives' coffee. I knew I probably shouldn't be hearing it so I didn't tell you until now."

I was the battalion executive officer. The battalion commander had given us the information on a confidential basis a few days before at an officers' meeting. The information had just this morning become official.

Despite my crestfallen reaction to seeing my news turning out to be no news, the wives' grapevine was a part of army life. The leader who was smart enough to make use of it found it an effective means for knowing what was going on when he perhaps could not find out directly.

Gyroscope was the term the Pentagon assigned to a plan for rotating whole units overseas during the Cold War. The idea was to avoid a stream of individual replacements coming and going, so as to keep the tactical units in Germany and Korea in a high state of training and readiness.

This would be our first move together for our family of six. Always before I had gone on ahead and the family would follow weeks or months later. So it was that a few months later, we found ourselves driving through a drizzle into New York City on the New Jersey Turnpike in traffic I had never before encountered. Gigantic semi-rigs were relentlessly bearing down on us from the rear while we were surrounded on all sides by vehicles hurtling along at about seventy miles an hour. Since then I have gotten used to freeway traffic, but that was my first experience and I remember that I wasn't happy. At least our household goods were in storage and the trauma of cleaning and passing the inspection of our erstwhile quarters was now behind us, and we were definitely on our way to Munich.

After spending a couple of days in a hotel near the Brooklyn Bridge, we got our final shots and prepared the station wagon for shipment. Late in the day we finally found ourselves, along with three small children and the baby, sitting in a giant warehouse on the Brooklyn docks while we waited for a bus to take us to Idlewild Airport. There we would embark on an overnight flight to Europe.

By this time my wife and I were only communicating in short, strained utterances. That was a long time ago, but I think now that the cause of the difficulty was a last-minute shipment of items she wanted to send to her mother in Denver.

Silently we rode to the airport. Silently we waited a long time to board the giant TWA "Connie" that would fly us to Germany.

Silently we boarded the aircraft. While Eloise shepherded the older children to their seats, I carried six-month-old Bruce and placed his bag of necessaries between my feet. The steward made an announcement that this was the last chance to stow any unneeded luggage in the hold. My wife came down the aisle selecting items to be taken and when she came to me she pointed to the bag between my feet and said, "Take that one."

I said nothing.

By the time we landed in Shannon, Ireland, about eight o'clock the next morning, poor Bruce was wet up to his neck for the lack of diapers. If it weren't for the kindness of others he would have been very hungry, too.

Arriving in Munich was something of an anticlimax. We were met by my counterpart from the unit we were relieving. He escorted us to our new quarters, which were all ready for us—even the refrigerator was stocked with enough food for the first few days. It had been a strange start for what turned out to be one of the most fulfilling and satisfying tours of our time in the Army. Fortunately, Eloise loved Army life as much as I did and we most often looked forward to the new experiences that lay ahead.

■

Like the Power of Angels
INEZ VALENTINE

The year was 1990. The month was June. I was visiting my daughter Annette and her family when they lived on Walton Lake. Annette had asked earlier to experience the power of angels.

One day the sun was shining brightly in the morning, but toward three or four o'clock the rain started to pour down like big buckets were being emptied on us from a dark sky. The rain continued to come down for thirty minutes. Then it stopped and jagged white strikes of lightening began, just a few at first, then more and more until every second another white strike would hit the water of Walton Lake. We were all huddled in the living room watching.

Jenny, Annette's daughter, went around turning off all the appliances. "Maybe it will ward off the strikes from hitting the house," she said.

The thunder was deafening and constant. Looking out at the lake we were terrified because the water of Walton Lake was boiling. I had never seen anything like this storm. The raging strikes seemed to be concentrated on the lake and nowhere else.

We were all chilled and shaking with fright, yet we couldn't take our eyes off the bright strikes lighting up the whole lake. I had heard that water is a perfect conductor of electricity, so I was thinking that it must be dangerous. Slowly, slowly the storm lessened until the tremendous display of power quit. We had had an unforgettable example of the power of angels.

∎

John Ong at age sixteen, 1943.

Turning Point
JOHN ONG

In the summer of 1980 I made plans to attend a three-week World Peace Assembly (WPA) on the campus of what was then Maharishi International University in Fairfield, Iowa. I rode my big Moto Guzzi motorcycle down from Milwaukee, Wisconsin, and spent the night at my sister's in Cedar Rapids prior to making the last leg of the journey the following day.

I had announced my plans to leave my cigarettes behind and use the restful and coherent environment to quit a habit of twenty-five years. I had heard incredible anecdotes concerning meditators who had simply "forgotten" to smoke, as if that were actually possible!

After breakfast that morning, I put one of my brother-in-law's Salem Lights (ugh!) in my shirt pocket and departed. At Kalona I pulled off the road, took out the cigarette and smoked it. Once on the WPA, after a day or two of only mild withdrawal, I began to have thoughts that perhaps, just perhaps, I might be able to stay quit. After two weeks I made an offhanded remark to someone that although I had stopped, I might start again at the end of the assembly. He said in effect, "Why don't you not do it?" And I didn't.

Every time I pass through Kalona, I point to the spot where I had my last cigarette. But this is the first time I have ever told the story of my Guardian Angel.

■

IV

RUN OVER BY KARMA

The Midnight Ride

HARRIET GLUBKA

It's midnight. I'm cozy in my warm bed. Suddenly the harsh ring of the telephone shatters the silence. I hope it's a wrong number. No, it's not a wrong number. A familiar voice at the other end says, "Mom, on the way home the car broke down near Rochester. Please come get us."

I shiver. "My car doesn't have enough gas to get to Rochester. I can't get gas at this hour."

Ron says, "That's OK, Mom. You can take my truck."

Silence at my end of the line.

Like a quick flash of lightning, the memory of learning to drive a car not too long before passes through my mind. First, the driver's training course and the resulting sore muscles from tension at the end of each session. Then, the big day—the official road test. (I passed.) Sore muscles from my weight training class were never this bad.

I'm jolted back to the phone call.

"Mom, are you there?"

"I guess so."

Long pause.

"Ron, I don't know how to drive a truck."

"You can do it, Mom. It's easy. The keys are on the dresser."

I seem to have no choice. After getting directions, finding the keys and wondering if I'm crazy or what, I drive up the hill, maneuvering the dangerous, curvy road which has seen many car accidents. There is a sudden drop-off on one side, a steep hill on the other side. It's pitch dark. Of course—no street lights on this mountainous Minnesota road. I pray as I go.

Suddenly, the truck lights go off and I experience the blackest darkness I've ever tried to see through. I'm petrified, but something tells me that I can't sit there frozen in the darkness. There might be a car coming from the opposite direction that won't see me in time to stop. I need to do something besides pray.

Somehow my hands are guided and I realize that Ron's CB radio has dropped onto the knob that switches the lights on—and off. I get the lights on and continue on my way. Eventually Ron, his wife and their little daughter come into my view. First we squeeze each other, then we squeeze into the truck's cab.

Believe me, I'm not sitting in the driver's seat.

■

Model T Ford

PAUL GODSMAN

One time a few years ago, I was riding on a Los Angeles freeway at night with my brother-in-law Verne. We were on the way back from a wonderful day on Catalina Island. We rode along with my wife and sister in the back. Observing the almost overwhelming sight of thousands of cars and the myriad lights of the city, Verne said, "I wonder if Henry Ford and Thomas Edison had any idea what tremendous changes their creations would bring to the world."

Reflecting on the changes they brought about I said, "I suppose those changes were more drastic for our parents' generation than ours."

For at the time I was born in 1919, such things as indoor plumbing, electric lighting, the radio, the automobile and the airplane were well established in this country. Of course, there was more to come in the form of television, computers, jets, rockets and the unleashed power of the atom, but these were mostly improvements on those original changes.

By the time I was fifteen and in high school, car ownership was to me a most desirable state of life. Freedom! Independence! Status! All these were symbolized by the ownership of a car.

So it was, after much wheedling, my parents relented and granted me permission to get a car. For the sum of fifteen dollars I became the possessor of a 1923 Ford touring car. It was what in those days was called a flivver. It was black and ungainly. I don't think the Model T was ever available in any other color. Though most of my friends had much better cars of more recent vintage, at least I now had wheels. It wasn't much good for getting dates with girls, so sometimes when I had that in mind I was allowed to use the family car, subject to many unwelcome restrictions, of course.

The first thing I did with that jalopy was to remove the touring body, leaving the dashboard, windshield and seat over the gas tank. I bolted on a makeshift platform to carry things behind the seat. Later on, I under-slung the suspension to make it ride closer to the ground. As I look back, I can see that it was a pretty dangerous contraption, but at that time my mind did not run to safety consciousness and I whiled away many beguiling hours working on that car. I drove it some too—to school and sometimes to the mountains.

One memory I have is using it as a smoke generator. By drilling a small hole into the front of the exhaust manifold and running a copper tube from a funnel on the dashboard, dense white clouds of blinding smoke could be produced while driving and pouring kerosene into the funnel. Fortunately no harm came of that. I think that I also installed one of the first seat belts. While going around corners, there was a tendency to slide off the seat. After one near-accident, I rigged a belt to hold my body on my perch, as well as anyone else who was bold enough to ride with me.

Leaving home to join the Army, I left that car sitting in my grandmother's garage along with a clutter of wheels and parts. When I returned at the end of the war, they were all gone. I asked my grandmother about it, but she replied, "I donated it to the scrap drive." She never had been happy about having that mess in her garage. There were no new cars on the market yet. So I shopped around and got a second-hand 1942 Ford convertible which I found befitting of my new lifestyle as a college student on the GI Bill.

There have been many cars since then. Though they all have their share of memories, that first old "Tin Lizzie" is still my favorite.

■

The Ride

HOSHEA LOVE

I have just trudged through an acre of freshly plowed ground on my way home. I feel like a soldier staggering out of a battlefield, finally making it to safety. Chain link gates and a watchdog greet me. I growl at Tish, telling her to shut up as I unlock the gates. I'm home! I don't want to be bothered or seen. I know every squeaky board in the floor. Stealthily I pick my way to my room. It's about 4:00 a.m. I'm tired—just want a cozy, comfortable bed. As the blankets fold around me, I drift into the darkness of deep sleep.

The next day is bright and clear, a late-summer Sunday morning. I unfold myself from the warm embrace of my blankets and slowly lift myself from bed. PAIN! Aaahh! Just over the right hip in my lower back and below my right knee. My shirt has blood on it, and a pant leg is torn where my leg is bruised. Breathing is heavy and labored; all my intestines feel as if they've been pushed to one side. Folding my arms across my belly, I carefully walk to the kitchen, where Mom and Dad are busily preparing for breakfast. Being careful not to draw special attention, I settle into a chair, situated so that both my folks will pass me at about the same time. When they do, I take a labored breath, and coolly say, "Guess what happened last night?"

My parents were good folks. And I was blessed, because they gave me the freedom to come and go as I pleased. I'm sure I was a mystery to them at times. Since they trusted me, I tried not to cause them any problems.

But last night had been strange for me. I had gone to a dance in our town and had a good time, but an unsettled feeling had begun annoying me. I couldn't figure out why, but after the dance I didn't feel much like going home. I didn't have a date, so I was free to do whatever I wanted. I decided to go for a ride.

My car was like a part of me. If you scratched her, I would bleed. Two-and-a-half years earlier I had special-ordered her from Detroit with the biggest engine-transmission combination available: a 1959 two-door Ford station wagon, baby-blue sides with a white top and hood. She had bench-type seats with no seat belts; they weren't required at that time. I customized her for high-speed cruising with a dropped front-end, special street tires, and straight exhaust pipes that came out from under the rear axles. She sat like an arrow ready for flight.

That night, we move out easily. Destination: the mountains. I don't give much thought to the ride until we reach Look Out Point, a high place where hang-gliders gather to test their flying skills.

Gravel crunches under the tires as the car rolls to a stop just before the rock wall. I get out and walk, enjoying the solitude and fresh night air. It's quiet with a slight breeze. You can smell the earthiness, the mesquite and sage, and hear sounds of wild critters here and there. This place is comforting, but a moody kind of feeling is still with me.

Thoughts lazily meandering... a small-town kid, not yet twenty-one, wrestling the need for direction. I suppose this is the underlying agitation feeding my uneasiness. My exposure to a great variety of places and experiences has left me with many bottom-line questions about life. I know that many folks are manipulated by their addictions to habits and ideas and their attachments to one thing or another, and few seem happy. I suppose I'm that way too.

I feel the urge to lie on top of the rock wall and gaze into the black sky, bedecked with a crescent moon and sister stars. I don't know how long I lie there, lost in reverie. Like a shooting star, a thought comes whispering, "It's time to go."

Swinging my legs off the wall, I amble over to the car, slide behind the wheel and turn the key. God, she sounds good, purring like a kitten. We're a fusion of oneness when we're cruising.

As we turn to leave, I feel the pebbly surface of the ground beneath us. The sound from the tires indicates a transition from gravel to pavement, hinting of a change in mood.

Thoughts are funny things. They come from nowhere, creating a world of activity in your mind. And across the screen of your consciousness, ideas, calculations, sights and sounds—each having a fluid translucent kind of form—dance and intertwine in such a way as to gather you up into a world, just beyond real.

We reach the bottom of the mountain in record time. The thrill of that ride gives me a high, like an addict. My addiction? Speed and the love for challenging corners. At the stop sign we turn south, homeward bound.

I mash on the throttle. Fence posts, trees and mailboxes whizzing by begin to blur as the needle creeps towards seventy. Cruising. Three hundred fifty-two horses under the hood. What a thrill it is to let them loose at times. The dancing forms in my head indicate that tonight is prime time. No cars, open road ahead—straight like an arrow. Thoughts flashing, like light beams overlapping. The needle shoots towards ninety. The burst of speed smacks me back into the seat. No side roads, no police cruising. At this early-morning hour all is clear—ninety-five, ninety-six, ninety-eight . . . .

ALERT! Our turning place, a side road ahead. Foot off the throttle.

Coasting. Yeah. Needle descending, ninety, eighty, seventy. Half a mile more. No problem. We'll hit the corner about fifty, negotiate and master it. We can do it! A right-angle turn, we'll make it like a curve. Headlights spot the turn.

What's that! NEW GRAVEL! Thoughts flash, calculating surface, slippery, turn unsafe. STRATEGY? Corner profile—two-way lanes intersecting, a small island, side exit. A stop sign—DO NOT ENTER. Take it, QUICK! TURN! Gravel scattering, tires sliding. CRANK the wheel, TOO FAST—off-balance—NO CONTROL!

Swished to the middle of the seat, like a passenger, I'm looking through the windshield. Headlights flash. A glimpse of road. We're in the air! Quietness, blurring, distortions—like being inside a bubble—drifting. It's curious how inside a moment, a split second, eternity replaces time and slow motion seems to cancel the power of gravity.

KERUNCH! A sound like a crisp cracker in somebody's mouth. SILENCE. Stillness. Pain gnawing at my back. Eyelids open. Darkness, Stygian black. Damn! I'm alive, on my back, on the floor, crumpled up against the firewall. Ugh! My head, crammed under the glove compartment. My legs, under the instrument panel and over the steering wheel. Damn! I hate causing my folks a problem.

Like a magician pulling a bunny out of the hat, I pull myself off the floor, out from under the dash, push the driver side door open, and stumble into the street. I look up and around. The feeling is strange. It's quiet, like being inside the observatory at Griffith Park, in the planetarium room where they simulate the heavens and the movement of the stars. The atmosphere seems surreal, like I'm in a dream. The car, like a dive-bomber sticking out of the ground. My hubcaps, somebody might steal 'em. I can't get to them all. One wheel's tucked underneath.

Let's go home. Let's trot. It's only a mile or so. Let's take the shortcut across the field. Yeah ! The car's insured—full coverage.

The next day my dad and I approached the scene of the accident. Of all the trees along the roadside, I thought it odd that a profusion of olives blanketed the ground under only one old olive tree. But when we got there, I saw at its base, crunched up like an accordion, my car. Then I knew about the olives.

The repairman had to stretch the frame of that car three different ways to get it straight again. I suppose that three-way stretch has symbolic meaning. Because, since that fateful event at the old olive tree, three things have no longer manipulated me—attachment to things, speed and the love for challenging corners.

■

Cielle Kollander at age ten, standing in front of the family car, California, 1950.

Silver Streaks and Fiery Dragons

CIELLE KOLLANDER

"The world is an exciting place out there,"
they hum and whisper—
these shiny streaks.
This up-side-down "v"
dissolving mysteriously
into nothing.
"There are wondrous things out there
in that nothing
in that nowhere.
Oceans, skies, mountains, colors, music, trees, animals—
and fantastic things that don't have a name.
Even a circus maybe?"
they hum and whisper,
whisper and hum
their silvery story at me.

Nobody you knew had ever seen them—those magical mysteries. But I knew they were out there. Somewhere. I knew magical stuff really happened. All the time. "She has such an imagination." They would laugh at me. It was true. Not only my beloved tracks that whispered it, and the rushing trains, but my favorite stories on the radio told me all about it. They all told me it was so.

Then of course there were those extra-shiny pictures in the *National Geographic* that really clinched it. It was out there. I knew it.

Now the *National Geographic* must have been a special thing. Different from anything else at our house. Mostly yellow. Shiny and heavy. Thicker and smaller than all the other magazines. From what I could tell, they must have been expensive, so they got *respect*—a word my father liked a lot. I wasn't quite sure how you got the magazine, but I think you had to be invited into a special club or something. You had to be very careful with them. And of course you would *never* throw one away. So they ended up in neat stacks everywhere. Even piled under our beds.

You would never get to go to these places, and see all this amazing stuff yourself, though. Not unless you could do something very brave I guess. Like give up everything you knew, and just go. Maybe just get on that train. Run away. Running away was never far from my mind then. I thought about it and made plans. A lot.

But maybe if you waited long enough, one of the grown-ups—somebody you had to obey—would take you. Maybe they would finally say, "Wanna go on the train to a place you've never been?" Oh boy. But no. Grown-ups were always too busy. Too serious. And *much* too tired.

Besides, how could *they* know this secret stuff? They didn't even know you. And you were right here, right in the same family, right in the same house. Oh well. Oh well.

Now my brother Stevie and I, we loved to walk the tracks not far from our house. Mostly we loved waving at the driver. Sometimes he would toot the train whistle, just for us. I just loved the cabooses. I wanted my very own caboose to live in when I grew up.

We had toy trains with real alcohol steam engines at our house. My dad and brother sorta owned them. I could never figure out why it was only OK for men and boys. Dolls were for girls and trains were for boys. I didn't like that one bit. I loved my dolls, especially my little black baby-doll. But I loved trains just as much as any ol' boy ever did. Maybe more.

I wasn't allowed to go to the tracks alone yet. Even though, after all, I was almost eleven. My brother was two years and three months older, so I begged him to go with me. He loved them almost as much as I did, I think. We would walk right on top of the tracks. We'd walk that funny walk too. Remember? One foot up on the track and one foot down? Up. Down. Up. Down. Sometimes there were pennies squashed flatter than a pancake—flat almost as paper.

We were in the tunnel when we first felt the rumbling. We loved the tunnel's darkness and its light at each end. The air damp and cool. I loved to sing in there and just make wild sounds. It felt good to scream and hoot and sing really high like a whistle.

Oh no, the train was coming in the other-end of the tunnel. There it was. It was on us. How did this happen? Its whistling made strange things happen to my ears, vibrating and buzzy. And I could feel the pounding through my feet. The look on my brother's face and how he was beginning to squeeze my hand tight and drag at me let me know he was afraid.

We were running for our lives now, out toward the light. "Run fast and hang on to me for dear life!" A worried shout from my brother. He looked white. We had to get out of that tunnel fast. I was scared to death. I knew he was, too.

Well, when you're only ten, and it's that close all of a sudden, a train is like a dragon. A monster breathing fire down on you. A smoking giant. Pounding. Shaking the whole world and shouting:

"WATCH OUT. GET OUT OF MY WAY.
I'M COMING THROUGH.

I AM THE HEAVIEST
AND STRONGEST THING IN THE WORLD.
I AM FUN, YES,
BUT I AM DANGEROUS TOO WOO WOO!"

We finally made it out of the tunnel, shaking so hard we could hardly stand up. Scrambling, trying to find a place to hang onto, 'cause the steep, rocky banks fell into a canyon way down below. We dug our feet in and lay flat against the rocks.

Now I felt the air from those huge, speeding wheels. They began to suck at me—tugging, pulling hard. My brother's face was getting whiter by the minute. He was holding on to me so tight my hand was nearly wrenched off.

"Hold on tight, don't let go!" he screamed. The train was so loud and so close, we had to shout to hear ourselves.

This time, I was certain we were gonna die. I knew it. This time, we were gonna be pulled right under that train. And we were gonna die for sure. Why didn't we listen when daddy warned us to be careful? "Don't you play near those tracks if you hear anything coming, you kids, anything at all." He warned us a thousand times. Now he would find us here. Dead. Squashed flat like two paper pennies.

Choochoochoochoo . . . Choochoochoochoo . . . as the black, steaming monster rushed at us, the pull and the pounding was almost unbearable. Steam was flying out from every direction like hot, angry clouds. The blast of the whistle was deafening—it was so close—it made our ears hurt bad. My brother was shaking now and screaming again, but I could only see his mouth move. I couldn't hear a thing.

At that moment, I saw my grandfather, standing right there. Tall. Quiet. (Everyone loved him. He was a Cherokee Indian *and* a Cowboy.) This was not my imagination. See, he really was there. Papa had come to save us! But he was too late. He was all the way across the other side of the tracks. *Papa, Papa.* I was crying now. Oh, it was impossible.

But he just stood there looking at us. Quiet and strong. We stared back, scared out of our wits. But as he looked at us, and we looked back, I knew he had come to save us. We were going to be okay. Weren't we? He would never in a million years let anything happen to us. We knew that. So just seeing him there was enough. Standing quiet. Waiting for the train to pass.

The train was right at us, covering up our Papa except for the flickering in-between train cars. Then we couldn't see anything anymore, our heads were down. But we knew he was over there. *We've got to just hold on. Not let the train suck us under those huge iron wheels, and kill us. We can do it. We gotta.* My mind screaming a million miles an hour.

It went on for hours. Chugging and steaming and whistling. Pulling at us. God the pulling. And the rocks started sliding. Now we were sliding down toward the canyon. Our hands and knees bleeding. *Help us, God, don't let us die. Oh, God, please. Oh, Papa, don't let Stevie die.*

Well.

We didn't.

We didn't die.

Thank you, God.

Thank you, Stevie.

Oh, thank you, Papa.

Well, this was just about enough excitement and wonder for me, for a long, long time. All I wanted to do was hug my grandfather and never let go. My hero. He quietly wiped our tears, mopped the blood from our hands and knees, and picked me up in his huge, loving arms. Exhausted, I fell asleep as he took my brother's hand and silently walked us home.

■

My Cancer

FERN FAIRIEBELL FLESNER

I sit and watch the snow and wonder.
Why did this wonderful experience happen to me?
How can I tell it when I don't know what it was?
How can I explain to anyone this inner lifting of my spirit,
This feeling I can only call my bliss?
People—friends and doctors—looked at me as if I were from outer space
When I tried to tell them what this feeling was that took over my body and left me feeling all aglow inside.
It was so the opposite of what it was supposed to be.
I had this dreaded thing called cancer in my body;
It was like a blight.
I was surprised they found it and the Docs said it would not go away unless we fought with all the tools and drugs they always used.
I listened and I knew they were sincere.
But something inside me, somewhere, was not afraid.
I don't know why—I've always been the one to acquiesce, to go along with everything they said.
Peace and quiet left my soul and I struggled—what oh what to do?
My friends were listeners and tried to help. I knew no peace until I found a book about a man who loved his sickness and why not?
To me it had brought nothing but the best—so much love and a

better way of life.

My children showing love, unspoken all these years, now coming out—

The little things now shown in ways I never would have dreamed—

Devotion shown by attention to the smallest need,

Hands touching, patience, consideration—just for me.

I knew that it was there but now I saw it, felt it every day— shown by what my family did in every possible way.

How could I not love this thing called cancer?

It brought me lovely things and I found better ways to eat and live, to stop and hear a bird's song, to look at nature in a way I never had before, to value friendships and a smile from strangers.

A whole new world had opened up—

Of love I had never stopped to know—

Of friends who cared but never stopped to tell.

Now they came and made me realize that they were there for me all along.

So then the bliss came back.

Thank God, it all came back.

And I did only natural ways like different food and many other new and different things.

I prayed a lot to my guardian angels and to many friends and family gone before.

I felt them close and helpful and thought of joining them, not in any morbid way, but as a place of happiness and joy.

My son insisted that I get a check to find out just exactly where I stood.

And then it came—the news that it was gone—gone. At first it took my breath away.

I'd prayed and worked for this yet it just could not be true.

All sorts of feelings crowded in and I felt joy, joy, joy

And thanks to God.
And then a touch of sorrow for my bliss, but it has slipped and turned and left a sweet, sweet joy.
I realized I had just received a gift.
A time to see my life and my family in a different way.
A time to know my friends and all they had to give.
A time to hear and appreciate the songs of nature and love the sun so warm upon my face.
A knowing now that every moment counts and kind thoughts and family and friends are what make life a joy.
And most of all that love and love alone is what our lives are all about.

∎

Recovering
JOHN ONG

After a stroke, what happens? Half the body is impaired in its function and speech is garbled.

After the medical staff has done its prescribed procedures, monitoring vital signs and medicating and fluidizing the body, one waits for the healing to take over. Firstly, know that healing is miraculous and in no way connected with medication.

Physician heal thyself? That is the only way that he can do it! Well not quite—it also takes prayer and positive thoughts. Four people come by that Sunday, the day after my stroke, with affirmative ministry of prayer for healing. It is only later that you learn that others are pulling for you, both in and out of your presence.

By the next day the miracle begins—strength and movement start their return to the body. Oh, oh—cramping starts and I have to ask for the dreaded bedpan. More miraculousness—everything down there works just fine!

Karen, my occupational therapist, comes on Tuesday and we start developing my Activities For Daily Living (ADL). All praise to on High! I can use the facilities! I can wash myself! I can brush my teeth!

Life then becomes a succession of therapy sessions, Linda and her staff working on development of gross motor activities by way of physical therapy (a.k.a. pain and torture). Denise develops fine motor activities via occupational therapy and Sandy helps with speech and swallowing. (Sandy sees snags with sibilant sounds.)

Another succession is that of well-wishers—Harriet, Holly, Charles, my brother Richard and his friend Susan. My daughters Susan, Sarah, Rachel and Ruth arrive from far and wide—thank goodness the occasion for their reunion is not more somber. Also, my wife, Dian, is with me continually throughout, greatly speeding my recovery.

After the ninth day, all of the therapy goals have been met and I go home. My doctors and staff say that I have been lucky. I believe it.

My recovery came from support of nature, positive outlook, well wishes and prayer.

■

*Inez Valentine, age seventy-eight, holding her beloved
great-granddaughter, Estelle, age three months,
March 20, 1997, Pocatello, Idaho.*

The Ultimate Adventure
INEZ VALENTINE

When I was twenty-one I became very ill during the seventh month of my first pregnancy. The year was 1940. We were living in the basement apartment of Nick's uncle's barbershop and home. I had a bad cold that I couldn't seem to get rid of. After Nick left for work at midnight, I went to bed but woke up with a painful, throbbing headache. Taking aspirin didn't help. I was walking up and down the hallway at intervals throughout the night because I couldn't sleep.

Toward morning I started to have convulsions and drifted in and out of consciousness. Every time I had a convulsion I would bite my tongue. Blood was everywhere.

I heard Nick's uncle making a fire in the little monkey stove in the furnace room. This is the way he heated water for the barbershop. Barely able to stand, I opened the door to ask him to tell Nick's mother that I was ill. I was barely hanging on to consciousness.

Nick came home and I gave up immediately, going into convulsions. He took me to the hospital. I was there ten days. (At this point I had to stop writing because remembering how ill I was made me upset.) I remember only a few things during my stay in the hospital.

Now I come to the purpose of this story. I was out of my body, floating near the ceiling, looking down at my swollen body and thinking, "I'm so glad to be out of that." Each hand was a huge ball of gauze. I learned later that I was temporarily blinded from toxins and had been scratching my eyes.

From the ceiling I continued on through the building, going up and up. A beautiful golden light surrounded me. It was most pleasant, a Presence that was the most, the very most—the most wise, the most beautiful, the most loving, the most considerate, the most understanding. This Presence communicated with me through his spirit and said, "You have to go back."

I answered, "No, I don't want to go back. This is the place I want to be. It's beautiful and warm and very pleasant."

Then he showed me a photo of two sweet little girls saying, "These are your children." I looked at those beautiful girls and finally agreed to go back.

Instantly I was back in my body, miserable because every cell was screaming with pain. I lost consciousness. When I awakened, I was completely healed. My doctor told me later that it was a miracle that I was alive. The baby was born dead about two weeks after I left the hospital. After I lost the baby boy I weighed only seventy-eight pounds.

Throughout my life I have often remembered the Presence that communicated with me. In 1942 Annette was born and Rita in 1944. Years later my brother-in-law took a photo of my precious little girls. It was the photo that the Presence had shown me.

■

V

MEET THE TNT BUNCH

Maargaret Ashelman

MEET MARGARET ASHELMAN

Born in Shanghai, China, daughter of two American missionary-doctors, I arrived in the U.S. in time to live on a Navaho reservation during my college years and to see my children and grandchildren live in Africa, Japan and China, as well as several American states. Now I live simply in Iowa, where Canadian winds swoop down but at least allow us to gather twice daily with friends from all over the country and the world who also practice the Transcendental Meditation program. And to gather weekly with a small writing group who have cooked up this book in time for April Fool's day publication.

LIFTING SELF-ESTEEM

As the youngest member of a family of achievers, I didn't realize how wobbly my self-esteem was. Even though I was the only member of our three siblings who graduated from Swarthmore with high honors and was elected to Phi Beta Kappa, I quickly recall that my sister was a better dancer and my brother played a bass viol. I only played the piano and not that magnificently.

Writing and reading have been life-long passions—reading more than writing. I wrote a diary during the trip from Shanghai to New Haven, Connecticut, via Manila, Europe and England, but haven't kept a journal except briefly under the encouragement of a friend. Writing letters to family members has been part of the natural territory, because children and siblings have been scattered to Australia, Africa, Japan and China since their college days.

Only now as a great-grandmother do I confront—honestly and humbly—my fragile self-esteem. I used to put on a twelve-person dinner-party with place cards and elegant food (and no helper) or regularly cook a meal for grown children working at our family resort, but that came with the role of mothering. Writing helps me remember what I have accomplished in the past and has challenged me to look at some of my skills now.

Participating in the weekly assignment of writing on various topics fits neatly into what my astrological chart shows: that I'm comfortable being part of a group, and I'm comfortable writing. The group brings me a new, beloved family of contemporaries who offer companionship and nourish my self-esteem. Writers in this group also examine where they are on their life journeys—and record comments as individual and endearing as their beloved faces!

—*Margaret Ashelman*

Dorothy M. Beal

MEET DOROTHY M. BEAL

As Dotty Cooley I loved acting, drawing and reading. As Dorothy Mullenneaux I loved raising six kids, teaching Head Start and being a teacher of the Transcendental Meditation technique. As Mazee I loved playing with my ten grandchildren. Now as Dorothy Beal I am back to acting, writing and life with an adorable husband.

ASKING THE COSMIC QUESTIONS

I love getting together with our writing group. My words seem to flow more easily. Being able to read to them, enjoying their praise, and receiving their evaluations has helped enormously. Now I am remembering who I was and realizing that I still am.

I was startled to hear someone say, "I hope we can continue after the book." Continue? But we have only begun! We must continue. To explore what we felt in our past is but a bare beginning. We have not yet asked ourselves the big questions: "Who am I? What is my purpose in this lifetime?"

We must go on. Let us answer these questions in our writing. Why am I here when so many of my family and my friends have passed? What do I love? What do I believe? Why do I believe it? Let us all be pioneers, not merely in being alive at eighty but in truly living at eighty.

—Dorothy M. Beal

■

Fern Fairiebell Flesner

MEET FERN FAIRIEBELL FLESNER

I was born on the South Dakota prairie and grew up in the Black Hills. My first husband was killed in World War II, leaving me with three small children. I met Hal, my present husband, at the University of Illinois, where I was a young housemother providing badly needed rooms for veterans. While living in California for thirty years, our family grew with the adoption of a son and we were blessed with grandchildren and great-grandchildren. Hal and I came to live on the campus of Maharishi University of Management in 1986, where I have fulfilled my life-long dream of going to college. Our life on campus is active and happy among many loving people, all of whom are devoted to helping bring about a more peaceful world.

REMEMBERING THE PAST

I enjoyed writing about the past for many reasons. Mostly, I loved the company of people in my own age group because we have a lot in common. The Great Depression affected most of us in some way, and World War II touched all of our lives. Most enjoyable of all was remembering the little things, the chickens and pony and people that were a part of my daily life when I was small and lived on a farm. Perhaps I'd not have given them a second thought without this chance to probe my memories.

It's been an uplifting experience remembering with my friends. I hope my seven grandchildren, my eight great-grandchildren and my seven great-great-grandchildren will find my memories meaningful and will pass them on in our family.

—Fern Fairiebell Flesner

Harriet Glubka

MEET HARRIET GLUBKA

Harriet Glubka was born in 1918 and grew up on the Speltz family farm in southeastern Minnesota with her parents, six siblings, two dogs, seven cats, two horses, sixteen cows, and one bull. She and her husband, Addison, had five children. After being widowed at the age of fifty-one, she went back to school and earned a bachelor's degree in political science and a master's degree in educational psychology and counseling. At the age of sixty-eight she became a teacher of the Transcendental Meditation technique.

A PASSION FOR LEARNING

Being in our memoir writing class gave me the motivation to start writing again. The group consciousness effect of a class is powerful, adding a dimension that is not present when writing solo. My memory is stimulated to bring forth specifics of events long since forgotten. That helps me to get a broader perspective on my life. Focusing to put these memories into words is good exercise for my brain and gives me a feeling of being more alive. Having our teacher give expert guidance to improve writing skills makes the whole experience very satisfying in terms of learning, which has always been the passion of my life. I look forward to the weekly meetings. It's amazing to see the power writing has, to see how writing helps group members get in touch with old feelings and to become softer, more open people. I feel that this process has done the same for me. Hallelujah!

—Harriet Glubka

■

Paul Godsman

MEET PAUL GODSMAN

Born: November 14, 1919 in Burlington, Ontario, Canada.
Military Service: Colorado National Guard, 1936-41. Commissioned 2nd Lieutenant of Artillery, February 1941, and called to active duty. Volunteered for the Parachute Troops in October 1942 and served in the South Pacific and the Philippines with the 11th Airborne Division. Separated from the service in February 1946.
Marriage: Eloise Warshauer in May of 1948.
Education: Graduated from Denver University in 1948 on the GI Bill. Majored in political science and education.
Returned to active duty with the Army: Army of Occupation in Japan and the Korean War, 1949-51. Retired from the Army in 1964 with rank of Lieutenant Colonel.
Children: Carroll, Kathleen, John and Bruce.

SHEDDING EMOTIONAL BAGGAGE

The writing of these short pieces acted as a catharsis, bringing me to terms with unresolved attitudes about past events and people. The process of writing about past experiences has helped me to get rid of unnecessary emotional baggage. Being able to hear the stories of other members of the class was also a big boost. I am learning how much life is a shared experience. The generation that experienced such things as the Great Depression, World War II, the Korean War, the big bands and the baby boom have many stories—stories that are part of the heritage of those who are coming after us. It's important for us to write them down and pass them along.

—*Paul Godsman*

■

Cielle Kollander

MEET CIELLE KOLLANDER

The proud grandmommy of nine-year-old Teddy Eddy May, Cielle Kollander has lived a colorful life from preacher's kid to Las Vegas dancer. She was educated in the U.S., Europe and Asia. She is a recipient of two Gold Records and The National Poetry Award. Her short stories appear in the best selling series, *Chicken Soup for the Soul.* After miraculously surviving a catastrophic car accident, Cielle moved her home base to a spiritual community, smack in the middle of the cornfields of Iowa (as she likes to describe it), where she meditates twice a day in large groups for world peace. She travels the globe teaching WholeBodyPerformingArts Technologies™, and in her very spare time, she works on her autobiography, *Bad Girl Yogi: Confessions of a Rascal on The Path*, which at this rate, she says, should be out no later than 2025.

AWAKENING TO WHO I REALLY AM

Every day has been so full of itself. Hours of group meditation for world peace, the house and all its demands for order and beauty and, ah yes, making a living! Putting in the garden, picking up the fallen fruit, researching a sane insurance plan, calling my kids, who I miss so very much. And on and on it goes.

How to get to the things we were born to do? The things that make life truly worth living? The stuff that brings the bliss? Ah, that!

I had actually convinced myself I didn't have time even to write this piece, or to go to class. After all, my hand is swollen tight from yesterday's bee sting and the house painter is coming and wants to know today what colors I have chosen. With this early frost it's almost too cold to paint, so the pressure is on.

What a coward. Come on, Cielle, with all these excuses!

So I get up, don't even fold my blanket (now for Miss Perfectionist that's saying something) and come straight home from meditation. In this hour before the class, I am determined. I will go. I will have the assignment written. I will remember to double-space. I will get copies made for the group. Whew!

So this is what it takes to be the artist I am. To show up for myself. To take a stand for art. For bliss. For the pleasures life keeps quietly offering, in the midst of the madness that would use-me-up without a whim and not give-a-damn.

This class has awakened me, once again, to who I really am. I am a writer, an artist, a poet. And a musician. I deserve the indescribable bliss it creates in me—like nothing else. I want to feel this happiness, this stirring. I want it so much.

Finding a better insurance plan will never give me this. But my chores call and I must answer. I must pick up the fallen fruit before it rots. The bee hidden in the sweet juice stings because I'm in too much of a hurry to wear gloves or shoes. Why? When I am not in the bliss of doing what I love, I am rushing madly in search of it. So, you see, I must go in and write—or go mad.

So go. Write, Cielle. You're worth it. Nothing else is. One page. Enough. Copy. Go!

—*Cielle Kollander*

Hoshea Love

MEET HOSHEA LOVE

From my youth I have always had the unquestionable belief that I would live to be 120. Now that I am halfway there, it has occurred to me that humans by their inherent nature should live at least to that age. The knowledge we have today more than substantiates such a belief. Currently I am a full-time university student pursuing a sustainable-living major in the field of biology. One of my goals is to help develop sustainable communities among indigenous peoples. I am married and have three successful sons, each of whom has a family (collectively six grandchildren).

SHARING MEANS GROWING

A group of about fifteen gathered to learn about writing memoirs. This was the most congenial group I have attended in a very long time. I had the feeling that this was a cluster of friends with whom I would like to keep in touch on a regular basis. Usually I am very cautious about extending trust to another, so it was odd to feel trusting among so many people. For me it was a new experience of being nourished by friendliness.

Memoirs, milestones—yes, a turning point, an unfolding and a continuing. I'm influenced to follow through and write my life's experiences—the learning and observations. In this course I have been exposed to the value of sharing myself with others who are likewise sharing themselves. It has been an eye-opening experience. It's like a scene coming into focus, like actually seeing what you are looking at. Knowledge taking form in my mind's eye creates reflections on the screen of my consciousness that in time become recognizable.

What we remember has integrity and honesty because the memory is stored in the feelings from the time of the actual experience. It's a level of deep feeling and emotion that no longer has the original boundaries, but has become transcendent and therefore timeless.

I also want to write for my family, to help put into perspective our lives together and to explain why some things have happened the way they have. And especially, what has motivated me to make decisions and behave the way I have. I've come to realize that writing is also helping me to make sense of my own life as a human being and a member of this American society.

—Hoshea Love

John Ong

MEET JOHN ONG

Residences (in reverse order): Iowa, Wisconsin, California, Missouri, Utah, Military Service, Northern Rhodesia (Zambia), Spain.
Name (Ong): Origin Viking, out of England (means "respected old man" in Chinese).
Dharma: Integration (I want to know everything).
Progeny: Four daughters, fifteen grandchildren.

BEING OUR OWN HEROES

Thoreau once said that everyone should be his own hero. That resonates with me and my experience as a memoir writer. I was able to recall my past through mature, experienced and enlightened eyes, and to recast my history in enhanced form.

This is being a hero as applied to memoir writing: phrasing remembered events, accumulated over a lifetime, in a distinct idiom and having them shaped through loving criticism by my mentor-teacher and my fellow writers.

— *John Ong*

■

Inez Valentine

MEET INEZ VALENTINE

I was born in the mountains above a very small town just south of Pocatello, Idaho. My family moved to Pocatello when I was five, and I started voice training there when I was fifteen, singing parts in operettas and choirs. I married the day after I turned eighteen and have two daughters, three grandchildren and one great-granddaughter. I've also been an artist since age fifteen, when I started drawing pictures of my classmates. I've been teaching art classes and painting all my life, mostly oils but watercolors later on.

OPENING THE DOOR

First the class made me write, then I became aware of structure. Writing has opened the door to the subconscious. What to write about? Being in the group stimulates ideas and memories. I feel loved and supported.

—*Inez Valentine*

■

Susan R. Wilk

MEET SUSAN R. WILK

January 20, 1915—Born in Gauting, near Munich, Germany
1921-1932—Primary and secondary schools
1932-1934—Completed apprenticeship in dressmaking, one-and-a-half years at Meister Schule Fuer Mode (fashion school), Munich
1936—Ousted from Meister Schule Fuer Mode when Hitler made it illegal for anyone with Jewish blood to attend school or work in a public job; left Germany and stayed one-and-a-half years in Rome, Italy
1937—Back to Munich at Christmas time
November 9, 1938—*Kristallnacht* (the night the Nazis smashed windows of Jewish proprietors and all personal property was seized)
Early 1939—Left Germany to live with a family in Denmark; rest of family scattered to England, Germany and the U.S. until after the war
September 1939—Escaped by night in a fishing boat to Sweden when Hitler invaded Denmark; worked in Sweden as a fashion designer
1947—Arrived in New York and worked as a fashion designer
1961-1967—Established Susan Wilk Coordinates, children's fashions
1968-1972—Earned Bachelor of Science (Music), Hunter College
1974—Earned Master of Arts (Music), Queens College; since then, teach piano and recorder
1995-present—Residing in Fairfield, Iowa

SEEING MY LIFE UNFOLDING

My husband, Jerry Wilk, used to write a weekly report about Broadway plays and other American cultural events for Voice of America and German radio stations and newspapers. The German radio producer Joachim Preuss, from Sender Freies Berlin (SFB), would include my husband's report in his weekly radio show. Whenever I visited Berlin after my husband's death, Mr. Preuss would invite me to a performance at the opera, or we would meet for lunch or dinner.

On one such evening at the Opera Cafe, I was telling him and his girlfriend about Hitler's occupation of Denmark and my escape from Denmark to Sweden. Mr. Preuss said, "Mrs. Wilk, you should write your story." This was several years ago. Since that time I have been working on my family's and my own memoirs.

This past spring my daughter told me about a memoir-writing workshop. During the course, we were told to write spontaneously about some event or happening as it unfolded in our minds. After the course ended, I continued writing that way for a while until I thought I should get back to my family memoirs. Then judiciously and somewhat detached about the various happenings and events, I began seeing my life story unfolding as a whole and started writing from this vantage point.

—Susan R. Wilk

Printed in the United States
24721LVS00001B/94-120